3.03.   PEM

03. JUL 08

20 JUL 2019

WITHDRAWN

Books should be returned or renewed by the
last date stamped above

GAFF. Jackie

J 709.04   20th Century Art

1910·20

20TH CENTURY ART

1910-20

The BIRTH of ABSTRACT ART

A HISTORY OF MODERN ART

20TH CENTURY ART – 1910-20
was produced by

David West ☆ Children's Books
7 Princeton Court
55 Felsham Road
London SW15 1AZ

Picture Research: Brooks Krikler Research
Picture Editor: Carlotta Cooper

First published in Great Britain in 2000 by
Heinemann Library, Halley Court, Jordan Hill,
Oxford OX2 8EJ, a division of Reed Educational and
Professional Publishing Limited.

OXFORD MELBOURNE AUCKLAND
JOHANNESBURG BLANTYRE GABORONE
IBADAN PORTSMOUTH (NH) USA CHICAGO

04 03 02 01 00
10 9 8 7 6 5 4 3 2 1

ISBN 0 431 11601 6 (HB)
ISBN 0 431 11608 3 (PB)

British Library Cataloguing in Publication Data

Gaff, Jackie
1910-1920 The birth of abstract art - (Twentieth
century art)
1. Art, Modern - 20th century - Juvenile literature
I. Title
709' .041

Printed and bound in Italy

PHOTO CREDITS :
Abbreviations: t-top, m-middle, b-bottom, r-right, l-
left, c-centre.

Front cover & pages 6b, 10r, 11t, 22b & 26b -
Bridgeman Art Library © ADAGP, Paris & DACS,
London 2000. 3, 6t, 7m, 9b, 10l, 11b, 16t, 18t, 19m
& br, 21t & bl & 23 - AKG London. 4t, 7b, 15 & 26t
- Corbis. 4b - Tom Donovan Military Books. 5, 13t &
20 - Bridgeman Art Library © DACS 2000. 8t -
Alitalia. 9t - © Archivo Icongrafico, S.A/Corbis 14t -
Stapleton Collection UK/Bridgeman Art Library. 14b -
© Tate London 2000. 16b - Imperial War Museum,
London/Bridgeman Art Library. 18b - Stapleton
Collection UK/Bridgeman Art Library. 19bl - Corbis ©
ADAGP, Paris & DACS, London 2000. 21br - Mary
Evans Picture Library. 24m - Haags Gemeentemuseum,
Netherlands/Bridgeman Art Library. 24b, 29t & b -
Frank Spooner Pictures. 25t - Bridgeman Art Library
© 2000 Mondrian/Holtzman Trust c/o Beeldrecht,
Amsterdam, Holland & DACS, London. 27 - Stedelijk
Museum, Amsterdam, Netherlands/Bridgeman Art
Library. 25b, 28 & 29m - AKG London © DACS
2000.

*The dates in brackets after a person's name
give the years that he or she lived.
The date that follows a painting's title and the
artist's name, gives the year it was painted.
'C.' stands for circa, meaning about or
approximately.*

*An explanation of difficult words can be
found in the glossary on page 30.*

20TH CENTURY ART

1910-20

The BIRTH of ABSTRACT ART

A HISTORY OF MODERN ART

Jackie Gaff

Heinemann
LIBRARY

CONTENTS

A MATTER OF SCIENCE
Scientific discoveries had a huge impact in the 1910s. In 1911–13, British physicist Ernest Rutherford and the Dane Niels Bohr (above) showed that the atom is not the basic unit of matter, but a moving bundle of electrons and other particles. 'The disintegration of the atom,' wrote Kandinsky in 1913, 'was to me like the disintegration of the whole world.'

TURBULENT TIMES

Among the many events that shook the world in the years 1910–20, by far the most cataclysmic was World War I (1914–18). This was the first war to take place on land, at sea and in the air, and it was the most appalling the human race had ever experienced, resulting in the deaths of as many as 10 million soldiers and almost the same number of civilians.

In the world of art, the years 1910–20 saw the most dramatic development in the history of modern Western painting – the birth of total abstraction, or art in which no attempt is made to represent scenes, people or objects.

WHITE CIRCLE, *Alexander Rodchenko, 1918*
Totally abstract paintings are made up of lines, shapes and colours that exist for their own sake, not to describe or suggest something else. The first geometric abstract art was created in Russia just before World War I.

The leading pioneers of abstract art were Dutch-born Piet Mondrian (1872–1944), and Russian-born Kasimir Malevich (1878–1935) and Vasily Kandinsky (1866–1944). It was a friend of Kandinsky, the Swiss-German artist Paul Klee (1879–1940), who caught the mood of his generation when he said in 1915: 'The more terrifying the world becomes… the more art becomes abstract.'

TECHNOLOGY ON TRIAL
World War I was the first conflict in which aeroplanes and tanks were employed as weapons. Both were new inventions – the first powered flight had taken place in the USA in 1903, while the tank was invented in Britain and first went into action in September 1916.

CUBIST CONSTRUCTIONS

Although they didn't themselves choose to go down the path to total abstraction, Spaniard Pablo Picasso (1881–1973) and Frenchman Georges Braque (1882–1963) had laid the foundations for it in 1907 when they began developing the fragmented art style known as Cubism. Picasso and Braque went on exploring Cubism in the pre-war years, together with followers such as the Spanish-born artist Juan Gris (1887–1927).

Juan Gris was only 40 when he died of kidney failure in 1927.

GLASSES, NEWSPAPER AND A BOTTLE OF WINE
JUAN GRIS, 1913

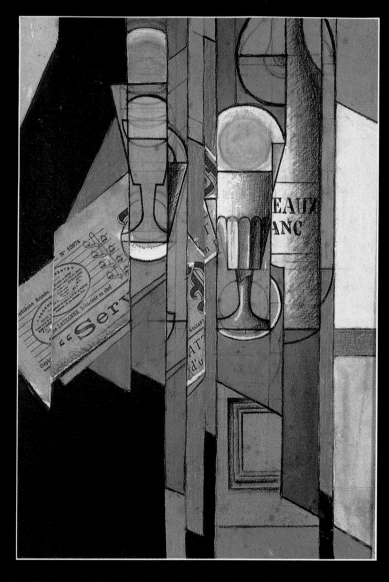

Gris moved from Spain to France in 1906 when he was 19, and rented a room in the same building as Picasso in the Parisian suburb of Montmartre. He didn't begin painting seriously until 1910, but was soon recognized as one of Picasso and Braque's most brilliant followers, quickly adopting new Cubist techniques such as collage and making them his own. In *Glasses, Newspaper and a Bottle of Wine* he employed a technique known as *papier collé* (French for 'glued paper') because the only collaged materials in it are pieces of paper such as newsprint. The Cubists also made three-dimensional collages that were halfway between a painting and a sculpture, using everything from fabric and string to wood and nails.

6

SHATTERED ILLUSIONS

Cubism was an entirely new, anti-naturalistic way of depicting people, objects and landscapes. Instead of the traditional, mirror-like illusion of three-dimensionality, the Cubists shattered their subjects and then put them back together to show them from all angles at once, like shards of broken glass.

GLUEING THE PIECES TOGETHER

By 1912 Picasso and Braque were entering a new stage of Cubism, partly as a reaction against their style becoming increasingly abstract. Rather than create an image by breaking down their subject, they now began to build it up by collaging real objects on to their canvases. In his *Still Life with Chair Caning* (1912), for instance, Picasso glued on a piece of oilcloth printed to look like the lattice-work caning on a chair seat. Picasso and Braque didn't invent collage – it had long been used in the home to make scrapbooks, for example – but they were the first people to make it an important part of fine art.

TUBULAR CUBISM
During his long working life, the French artist Fernand Léger (1881–1955) experimented with many different art styles, always making them his own. In the 1910s, he developed an individual form of Cubism and was nicknamed a 'tubist' because of his use of bold tubular shapes.

MODERN ART IN THE USA
The American photographer and art critic Alfred Stieglitz (1864–1946) played a vital role in introducing modern European art to the USA via his 291 Gallery, which opened on New York's Fifth Avenue in 1905. He also championed progressive American artists such as Arthur Dove (1880–1946) and Georgia O'Keeffe (1887–1986), who married Stieglitz in '24. The American general public was given its first major taste of modern art early in 1913, when the immensely influential Armory Show was held in New York City. More than 300,000 people paid to see hundreds of paintings and sculptures by American artists and avant-garde Europeans such as Picasso and Braque.

Stieglitz went on supporting avant-garde American artists until his death. This photograph was taken in the '30s, while he was hanging an exhibition of O'Keeffe's work.

CUBISM IN COLOUR

The palettes of Picasso, Braque and Gris were dominated by brown and grey in the pre-war years, but other artists were exploring a far more colourful form of Cubism. And while Picasso, Braque and Gris concentrated on still lifes, these colourful Cubists were excited by trying to capture the speed and energy of modern city life.

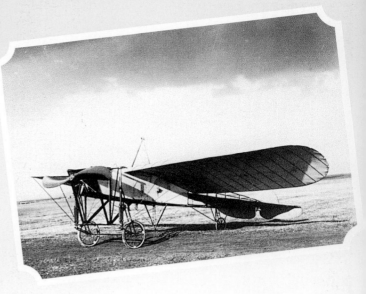

MODERN ART FOR A MODERN AGE

Beginning in 1909, the French artist Robert Delaunay (1885–1941) created a series of ever more colourful Cubist paintings of Paris and the things he considered the miracles of modern engineering. At the top of his list were aeroplanes and the 300-metre-high Eiffel Tower, which had become the world's tallest building when it was completed in 1889.

THE AGE OF FLIGHT
First achieved by the USA's Wright brothers in 1903, powered flight was one of the amazing scientific advances of the early 20th century. Flight was the essence of modernity and Robert Delaunay included aeroplanes in many of his paintings. His Homage to Blériot, 1914, was dedicated to the French aviator Louis Blériot, who in 1909 became the first person to fly across the Channel.

MAKING AN IMPRESSION
Robert Delaunay was a great admirer of the revolutionary artists of the 19th century, such as Claude Monet (1840–1926) and the Impressionists. Like them, he studied the science of light and colour and was fascinated by the law of simultaneous contrasts – this states that the differences between two colours appear at their greatest when they are placed next to each other (orange becomes more red when placed beside green, for example). In his own paintings, Delaunay used simultaneous contrasts to create movement and rhythm.

HAYSTACKS AT SUNSET, FROSTY WEATHER, *Claude Monet, 1891*

8

THE RUGBY TEAM
ROBERT DELAUNAY, 1912–13

Although they were among the first to create
totally abstract works, the Delaunays also carried
on making representational paintings. This one
is jam-packed with symbols of movement and
modernity – sport, an aeroplane, the Eiffel Tower
(top right) and a ferris wheel. Astra was the name
of an aircraft company, but also Latin for 'stars' –
Robert believed that the energy of colour linked
life on earth with the rest of the universe.

MARRIAGE OF MINDS

In 1910, Delaunay married the
Russian-born artist Sonia Delaunay-
Terk (1885–1979) and within two
years their interest in colour and
movement had led them to create
totally abstract paintings, in which
colour and shape existed solely for
their own sake, not to represent
objects. 'Colour is form and subject,'
Robert said about abstract paintings
such as his *Circular Forms* series,
'It is the sole theme that is developed.'
The Delaunays called their abstract
works 'pure paintings', but in 1913
the term Orphic Cubism (Orphism,
for short) was coined to describe
them by the French poet and art critic
Guillaume Apollinaire (1880–1918).
Apollinaire derived the word 'Orphic'
from Orpheus, the musician of ancient
Greek and Roman myth, whose music
was said to be so beautiful that even
rivers stopped flowing to listen to it.

9

*ARTISTIC INSIGHT
Apollinaire (right)
defined Orphism
as 'the art of
painting new
structures out
of elements that
have not been
borrowed from
the visual sphere,
but have been
created entire
by the artist
himself'.*

VASILY KANDINSKY

One of the three key figures in the development of abstract art, Kandinsky was born in Russia in 1866 and studied law and economics there. He was 30 when he decided to train as a painter and moved to the German city of Munich, at that time one of Europe's main artistic centres.

BLUE GROUP
In 1911, Kandinsky and the German artists Franz Marc (1880–1916) and Gabrielle Münter (1877–1962) founded an avant-garde group which they named Der Blaue Reiter (German for 'the blue rider'). The group held two exhibitions before being broken up by World War I.

MOMENTS OF TRUTH

Kandinsky said that he'd had several major turning points in his artistic life. The first was seeing one of Monet's series of paintings of haystacks (see page 8), which inspired him to take up art in 1896. The second took place in 1909, when he found an incredibly beautiful painting in his studio in which he could see 'nothing but shapes and colours'. He soon realized it was one of his own paintings, on its side, but the experience prompted him to explore abstraction.

COMPOSITION VII
VASILY KANDINSKY, 1913

Colours, shapes and lines collide and explode in this hugely energetic painting, in which Kandinsky's main theme was the death and rebirth of the universe. Kandinsky moved gradually towards total abstraction in the 1910s, and some of the paintings from this time have references to the real world – like the symbol for a boat with three oars in the bottom lefthand corner. After World War I, his style became more geometrical, with intersecting circles, triangles and squares.

COUNTRY PLEASURES
In 1909 Kandinsky and Gabrielle Münter moved into a second home in the village of Murnau, in the foothills of the Alps – this photograph of him was taken there a year later. Münter and Kandinsky were lovers and lived together until the war years.

THE MUSIC OF PAINTING

Kandinsky aimed to reveal spiritual truths through his art and believed that, like music, abstract art could set the soul vibrating, not just the eyes. 'Colour is the keyboard, the eyes are the hammers, the soul is the piano with many strings,' he wrote. He also developed a vocabulary of colour, identifying the unique properties of individual colours. Red gave 'the impression of a strong drum beat', for example, while yellow resounded 'like a high-pitched trumpet'.

MUSIC FOR THE MODERN AGE

Musicians were also breaking with the past, and one of the 20th century's most innovative composers was the Austrian Arnold Schoenberg (1874–1951). Schoenberg broke with tradition through his use of dissonance (lack of harmony) and atonality (music not written in a particular key). Most audiences were puzzled or even hostile at the time, but Kandinsky became an admirer and close friend after attending a concert in 1911. Schoenberg was a painter as well as a composer, and exhibited with Kandinsky's Der Blaue Reiter group.

Arnold Schoenberg

FUTURISM

The prize for the most vocal art movement of the period goes to Futurism, founded in 1909 by the Italian poet Filippo Tommaso Marinetti (1876–1944). Marinetti loathed the past and loved the modern – and nothing symbolized modernity more for him than speed!

SPEED FREAK
'We declare that the splendour of the world has been enriched with a new form of beauty, the beauty of speed,' wrote Marinetti. 'A racing car… is more beautiful than the Victory of Samothrace' (a famous ancient Greek sculpture).

OUT WITH THE OLD

Marinetti wanted to tear down museums and libraries – as monuments to traditional art and literature – and start again by celebrating the speed and dynamism of new inventions such as electricity, steam trains, steam ships, cars and aeroplanes. He glorified chaos and destruction, claiming that 'beauty now exists only in struggle' and describing war as 'the world's only hygiene'.

UNIQUE FORMS OF CONTINUITY IN SPACE
UMBERTO BOCCIONI, 1913

Boccioni was a sculptor as well as a painter and this dramatically striding figure is one of his most impressive works – as it sweeps forward, he explained, it carries 'blocks of atmosphere' along with it. In 1912, Boccioni visited Paris, where he saw and was influenced by the avant-garde sculptures of Picasso and Constantin Brancusi (1876–1957). He wanted to revitalize the 'mummified art' of the past, and make more of materials not traditionally used by sculptors – from glass and mirrors to electric lights and motors.

12

DYNAMISM OF A DOG ON A LEASH
GIACOMO BALLA, 1912

Balla wasn't interested in machines and violence, and his paintings were gently beautiful or funny, like this one. His depiction of the wagging tail and trotting legs of a dachshund is like a multiple-exposure photograph.

IN WITH THE NEW

Marinetti was a poet, not a painter, and the difficulty for the artists who joined the movement was finding a way to deal with his ideas visually. The leading Futurist artists were the Italians Giacomo Balla (1871–1958), Umberto Boccioni (1882–1916), Carlo Carrà (1881–1966), Luigi Russolo (1885–1947), Gino Severini (1883–1966) and architect Antonio Sant'Elia (1888–1916). Although their individual styles differed, these Futurists shared the search for a way to express speed and energy. They experimented with various art styles, including Cubism, along the way, and many of them ended up with an abstract, speeded-up version of Orphism.

GALLOPING HORSE, *Eadweard Muybridge, 1887*

MOVING PICTURES

Although some of them claimed to despise photography as a lesser art, many of the Futurists were influenced by the sequential photographs taken in the 1880s by Eadweard Muybridge (1830–1904) in Britain and Etienne-Jules Marey (1830–1903) in France. The Italian photographer Anton Giulio Bragaglia (1890–1960) was linked to the Futurists and experimented with long exposures of photographic film to create beautiful blurred images of moving people, such as a woman typing or a carpenter sawing. Bragaglia called these images 'photodynamic'.

VORTICISM

One of the spin-offs from Cubism and Futurism was a British group who called themselves Vorticists. The group exploded into life in July 1914 with the publication of a magazine called *BLAST*, but the outbreak of war rapidly put an end to their activities and by late 1915 they had scattered and gone their own ways.

COVER OF BLAST MAGAZINE, *Wyndham Lewis, 1915*
There were only two issues of BLAST – the second was in July 1915, a month after the one and only Vorticist exhibition.

THE MUD BATH
DAVID BOMBERG, *c.* 1913–14

Although British artist David Bomberg (1890–1957) turned down an invitation to join the group, the jagged semi-abstract shapes and energy of works like *The Mud Bath* are among the finest examples of the sort of thing the Vorticists were trying to achieve. Bomberg's painting may seem totally abstract at first, but it actually shows blue and white bathers leaping around a red rectangle of water. It was based on sketches made at public baths in the Whitechapel area of London's East End, where Bomberg grew up.

CLUB MEMBERSHIP

BLAST was edited by the British writer and painter Wyndham Lewis (1882–1957) and the first issue contained a manifesto signed by Lewis and several other avant-garde artists, including Britons Jessica Dismorr (1885–1939), William Roberts (1895–1980) and Edward Wadsworth (1889–1949), Frenchman Henri Gaudier-Brzeska (1891–1915) and the American poet Ezra Pound (1885–1972).

DEEP AND MEANINGFUL

Although, like the Orphists and the Futurists, the Vorticists aimed to celebrate the energy of modern life through abstract and semi-abstract art, their style was far more jagged. Pound, who claimed to have invented the group's name, highlighted the main difference when he described Futurism as 'a spreading, or surface art, as opposed to Vorticism, which is intensive' (by which he meant concentrated, with a sense of depth). The group's name was derived from the word 'vortex', meaning a whirling movement, and looking at a Vorticist painting can be like peering into a deep abyss or a black hole in space.

ARTISTS AT WAR

The outbreak of World War I in August 1914 shattered the artistic communities of European cities such as Paris and Munich. Some artists belonged to neutral nations and did not fight, while others joined up or were conscripted. Many died, including the Futurists Boccioni and Sant'Elia, the Vorticist Gaudier-Brzeska, and Franz Marc, the cofounder of Der Blaue Reiter.

LOST IN ACTION
Marc was killed at the Battle of Verdun in March 1916.

A BATTERY SHELLED, WYNDHAM LEWIS, 1919

Three officers stand on the sidelines while their men work to clear the aftermath of a bomb attack. Lewis was working from first-hand experience, having served as a gunner before becoming an official war artist in 1917.

Lewis toned down his abstract Vorticist style during the war not only in response to official restrictions, but because of his experiences. 'The geometrics which had interested me so before, I now felt were bleak and empty,' he said.

UPHOLD OUR
HONOR

FIGHT
FOR
US

JOIN
ARMY·NAVY·MARINES

ARTISTS AT THE FRONT

Many of the finest artistic responses to the horror of the war came after the peace of 1918, since only official war artists could work at the front – ordinary soldiers couldn't just stop fighting, put up an easel and start to paint. Australia, Britain, Canada and the USA set up official war artist schemes to provide propaganda during the war and to act as a national record afterwards. Women were employed as official artists on the home front, while men were drawn from the ranks of those who were either too old for active duty or who'd been injured and sent home.

POSTER PERSUASION
Many artists produced propaganda posters persuading men to sign up and fight.

PAINTING PART OF THE PICTURE

One drawback of these schemes were the restrictions placed on official war artists. In Britain, for example, paintings had to be accessible, which meant that total abstraction was out of the question. The War Office also placed a veto on showing corpses.

TERROR IN THE TRENCHES
World War I's massive toll of more than 10 million dead was largely due to the unleashing of horrifying new weapons and the slowness of military commanders to respond to new inventions. Soldiers in the trenches suffered the first poison gas attacks and the first use of flame-throwers. Bombs were dropped on them from aeroplanes for the first time, and thousands faced machine-gun fire from the newly invented tank, armed only with bayonets.

17

British front line, Battle of the Somme, 1916

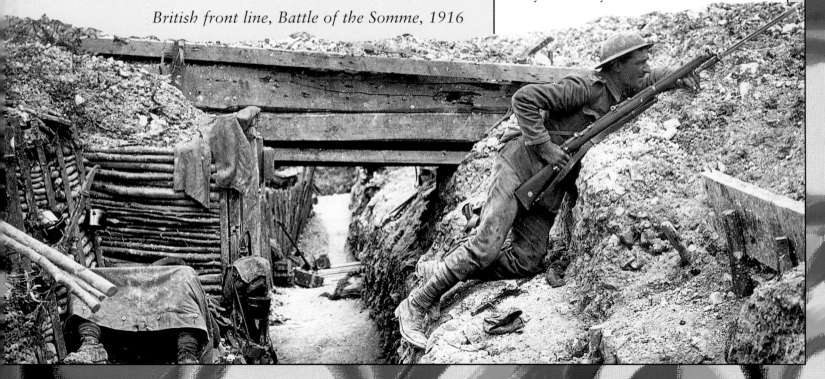

DADA

Anti-art,
anti-sense,
anti-morality,
anti-politics, anti-
war – Dada was
anti-everything!

WORLD AT WAR

The unspeakable brutality
of the war created a massive
sense of disillusionment
with the governments and
society responsible for
waging it. Dada was an
expression of disgust at the
so-called civilization that had
produced such barbarity. Its tools were chaos
and absurdity, and it deliberately subverted
all the arts – from music and poetry, to
painting and performance.

DADA ON SHOW
*In the final stages of the war, Dada took off in
German artistic centres such as Berlin, where this
photograph was taken in 1920. Hanging from the
gallery ceiling is a dummy dressed in a German
officer's uniform, with the head of a pig and a placard
that reads 'Hanged by the Revolution'.*

SWISS EYE OF THE STORM

The neutral country of Switzerland became a refuge for a number of
avant-garde writers and artists during the war, and European Dada
was born there in Zurich, in 1916. Its founders included
the German Hugo Ball (1886–1927),
Frenchman Hans Arp (1887–1966) and
the Romanian Tristan Tzara (1896–1963).

MAN OF MANY TALENTS
*One of the ringleaders of New York Dada was
American Man Ray – a painter, photographer, sculptor and
film-maker. In 1921 he moved to Paris, where his first Dada
event involved completely filling a gallery with balloons,
which viewers had to pop to find the art inside.*

18

FOUNTAIN
MARCEL DUCHAMP, 1917

A urinal laid on its back and signed R. Mutt – is this art? Few people thought so at the time, and many people would ask the same question today. Duchamp deliberately used ready-made objects like this to challenge artistic conventions. In doing so, he flung wide the boundaries of art and made it possible for ideas to be as important as the act of physical creation. Technical skill was no longer the be-all and end-all. Choosing an object for display could be equally significant – what mattered were the ideas.

MAKING A MUTT?
'Whether Mr Mutt has made the fountain with his own hands or not is without importance,' said Duchamp. *'He chose it... he created a new thought for this object.'*

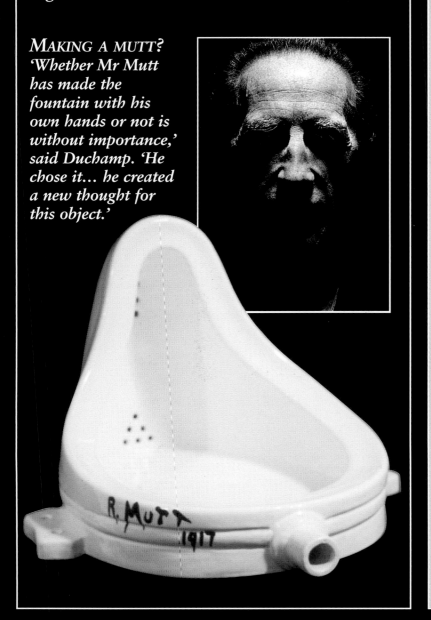

SCATTERING CHAOS

While Dada spread through Europe like wildfire, it developed independently in New York, where it was masterminded by French-born Marcel Duchamp (1887–1968) and Francis Picabia (1879–1953), plus American Man Ray (1890–1977). Dada's focus on chaos and absurdity had a huge impact on 20th-century art, spawning a number of important movements, including the dreamlike Surrealism of the '20s and '30s.

THEATRE OF THE ABSURD
The heart of Zurich Dada was Hugo Ball's nightclub, the Cabaret Voltaire. 'Happenings' there included dressing up to the nines to chant nonsense poems such as Ball's 'Karawane', which went 'zimzim urallala zimzim zanzibar...' Often the poems were drowned out by noise music produced by thumping drums, bottles and anything else that was handy.

Hugo Ball reciting 'Karawane' in 1916.

DE CHIRICO'S METAPHYSICAL PAINTING

The mysterious and dreamlike paintings of the Greek-born Italian Giorgio de Chirico (1888–1978) were almost as bizarre as the Dadaists' creations. And like Dada, his style was also to influence the birth of Surrealism in the '20s.

De Chirico called his art style Metaphysical Painting, using the word 'metaphysical' loosely to mean enigmatic or puzzling, or to describe the sense of alienation from reality in works whose effect was strange and sometimes shockingly sinister.

MELANCHOLY
GIORGIO DE CHIRICO, C. 1912

De Chirico painted mysteriously empty city squares like this one, edged by buildings and arcades (rows of arches) and striped by long, menacing shadows. Often there are no people, just classical statues or faceless dummies, like the ones used by dressmakers. The perspective is exaggerated or twisted, as in this work, where the statue is tilted even though the ground is flat. There's a strange sense of time being out of joint, too – is the painting set in the past, the present or the future? The buildings suggest the past, but in many paintings a tiny steam train puffs across the distant horizon. Sometimes de Chirico's images simply express sadness and loneliness, but at others there are strong feelings of fear and isolation.

LEARNING FROM THE PAST

De Chirico was unimpressed by Cubism and Futurism. Instead of turning his back on history, he embraced the classical art of Greek and Roman times. Rather than follow Picasso and Braque in breaking with the mirror-like illusion of three-dimensionality, he adapted and twisted the laws of perspective.

IN THE FRAME De Chirico was lionized by the Surrealists for the paintings he did during the 1910s.

MEETING OF METAPHYSICAL MINDS

De Chirico began developing his style when living in Paris in the early 1910s. After the war broke out he was conscripted into the Italian army and posted to the city of Ferrara in northern Italy, where he later suffered some sort of nervous breakdown. In 1917, while he was in hospital in Ferrara, de Chirico met Carlo Carrà, whose faith in the art of the past had been restored in the years since he'd originally signed up with the Futurists. Although their friendship was shortlived – it ended after a quarrel in 1919 – Carrà was an immediate convert to de Chirico's style and helped him to launch Metaphysical Painting as an art movement.

THE STUFF OF DREAMS With his fairy-tale images of lovers floating through the air and flying horses, another artist who influenced the Surrealists was Russian-born Marc Chagall (1887–1985).

MEASURES OF LONELINESS

The shift from farming to factories brought about by the Industrial Revolution of the 19th century had sparked the rapid growth of cities and towns. Alongside this had arisen the idea of the city as a place of alienation – somewhere you are alone even in a crowd. This sense pervades de Chirico's paintings and in literature it was expressed by the American-born Briton T.S. Eliot (1888–1965) in his great poem *The Waste Land*. Loaded with references to the literature of the past, the poem also questions the values of the present.

T.S. Eliot's The Waste Land *caused an uproar when it was published in 1922, with some critics calling it a masterpiece and others, a hoax.*

MODIGLIANI

Another artist with a love for the great works of the past was Amedeo Modigliani (1884–1920). Born in Italy, he settled in Paris in 1906 and spent the rest of his short life there.

BOHEMIAN RHAPSODY

Shortly after arriving in Paris Modigliani moved to the Montparnasse district, whose bars and nightclubs were, along with those of nearby Montmartre, the centre of bohemian Paris in the early 20th century. Modigliani threw himself into the decadent bohemian lifestyle with the same passion with which he pursued art. Addicted to drugs and alcohol, he said, 'I am going to drink myself to death' – and almost did. Weakened by his way of life, he was killed by a combination of pneumonia and tubercular meningitis.

PUTTING WOMEN IN THE PICTURE
Marevna was the nickname of the Russian-born painter Maria Vorobyov (1892–1984), given to her after she left Russia to study painting in Italy and France. During the 1910s, she moved in the same bohemian circles as Modigliani, and she painted this portrait in the '60s in memory of the friendships of that time.

HOMAGE TO FRIENDS FROM MONTPARNASSE, *Marevna, 1961*

JEANNE HEBUTERNE
Amedeo modigliani, 1919

Modigliani had numerous lovers and met the woman portrayed in this beautiful painting in July 1917. Jeanne had a child by him late in 1918, and was pregnant with a second when this portrait was painted. She was devoted to Modigliani and was still pregnant when she committed suicide by throwing herself out of a fifth-floor window two days after his death. Although inspired by the art of the past, Modigliani did not want to depict the real world. Instead he sought to express more spiritual and universal themes. Rather than make Jeanne's personality the chief subject of this painting – her expression is blank and her pale blue eyes are empty – Modigliani transformed her into a symbol of sad resignation.

On the left of the painting are Marevna and Marika, the daughter she had by her lover the Mexican artist Diego Rivera (1886–1957), with Rivera behind Marevna's head. In the centre is Modigliani, with Jeanne Hébuterne tucked behind his raised glass. Marevna also described the difficulties faced by women artists in those days: 'For a man the problem is easier to solve: he nearly always has a woman, wife or mistress, who earns money… She is devoted, and sacrifices herself until the man becomes celebrated.'

STUDENT OF A MODERN MASTER

Modigliani's finest works were the beautiful portraits and nudes he painted in the last five years of his life. He was influenced by the simplified forms of the sculptor Constantin Brancusi, whom he met in 1909, and had focussed mainly on sculpture until the outbreak of war ended his supply of materials and forced him to return to painting and drawing.

HEIR TO AN OLD MASTER

The uniqueness of Modigliani's style lay in the simple, elongated elegance of his depictions of women. The great 15th-century Italian painter Sandro Botticelli (*c.* 1445–1510) portrayed women with similar grace, and Modigliani is often described as his artistic heir.

SELF-PORTRAIT, 1920
Modigliani was a fine draughtsman and could capture his subject with a few simple strokes of pencil.

23

PIET MONDRIAN

The Dutch-born artist Piet Mondrian (1872–1944) was one of the three key figures in the development of total abstraction, matched in importance only by Kandinsky, and the Russian Kasimir Malevich (1878–1935).

DEAD END STREET

Mondrian was 40 when he arrived in Paris in 1912, and his subjects up until then had mainly been landscapes. He experimented with Cubism for a while, but was soon saying that it was 'not developing abstraction towards its own goal, the expression of pure reality'.

ROAD TO ENLIGHTENMENT

Like Kandinsky, Mondrian was a kind of early 20th-century New Ager, searching for a way to make art that would rise above the material world and express universal truths. He talked about art providing 'a transition to the finer regions, which I shall call the spiritual realm'.

COMPOSITION WITH RED, BLUE AND YELLOW
PIET MONDRIAN, 1930

For Mondrian, the pure colours and straight horizontal and vertical lines of his abstract paintings were an expression of the absolute harmony of the universe. Influenced by the mystical philosophies of his day, he believed that his horizontal and vertical grids achieved a balance between such things as feminine and masculine, negative and positive, and static and dynamic. Straight lines weren't his only passion, though – he was also a jazz fanatic who loved dancing!

PORTRAIT OF PIET MONDRIAN, M. *Elout-Drabbe, 1915*

24

FINDING A NEW DIRECTION

Mondrian went back to the Netherlands in 1914 to visit his sick father and was prevented from returning to Paris by the outbreak of the war. It was during this time that his paintings became increasingly abstract and he discovered his own individual style. By the early '20s he had arrived at the totally abstract, geometric style that he continued to explore until his death – no shapes apart from the square and the rectangle, and no colour apart from the three primaries (red, yellow and blue), plus black and white and, occasionally, grey.

25

LIE OF THE LAND
Mondrian's love of horizontal and vertical lines derived in part from the flatness of the Dutch landscape, crisscrossed by its grid of canals.

SETTING A STYLE FOR LIVING

In 1915, Mondrian met the Dutch artist and writer Theo van Doesburg (1883–1931) and converted him to geometric abstraction. Two years later van Doesburg founded a magazine and a group of artists and architects. He named them both De Stijl (Dutch for 'the style'), and they were hugely influential in launching a new, pared-down style of design in which simple geometric shapes were used for everything from furniture to houses.

DESIGN FOR UNIVERSITY HALL, *Theo van Doesburg, 1923*

MALEVICH & SUPREMATISM

The first totally abstract geometric painting was a simple black square on a white background, and the artist who made it was the Russian Kasimir Malevich. Although Malevich claimed to have created the work in 1913, the exact date cannot be proved and the first time it was seen in public was at an exhibition that was held in December 1915 in the Russian city of St Petersburg.

REACHING HIGHER GROUND

Malevich showed 39 abstract works at this exhibition, all composed of flat geometric shapes on plain backgrounds. He named his radical new style Suprematism, deriving the term from the word supremacy, meaning 'the state of being supreme or of utmost importance'.

REACHING FOR THE STARS
Launched in 1926, the first liquid-fuel rocket was designed by American Robert Goddard (above). Malevich was fascinated by the idea of space travel and the work of the Russian pioneer of space science, Konstantin Tsiolkovsky.

26

LEADING LIGHTS

Other leaders of the Russian avant-garde art in the pre-war years included Natalia Goncharova (1881–1962) and her lifelong partner Mikhail Larionov (1881–1964). Like Malevich, in the early 1910s Goncharova and Larionov worked in a style known as Cubo-Futurism, because it combined Cubist fragmentation of form with the Futurist fascination with speed and modern city life. All three artists also wanted to develop styles that depended less on Western European influences, but which drew instead on Eastern traditions such as folk art and religious icon paintings. In 1915 Goncharova and Larionov left Russia, settling in Paris in 1919.

THE CYCLIST, *Natalia Goncharova, 1912–13*

UNTITLED (SUPREMATIST PAINTING)
Kasimir Malevich, 1915

Malevich said that these kinds of coloured geometric forms on their simple white background transported him 'into an endless emptiness, where all around you sense the creative nodes of the universe'.

PURITY OF FORM

Malevich had experimented with Cubism and Futurism before pioneering Suprematism, but he'd grown dissatisfied with the way they still carried what he described as 'the burden' of representing objects. If his art was to be non-representational, Malevich had to find images that don't exist in the natural world. This was where geometry came in – pure geometric shapes such as squares and rectangles do not exist in nature, only in our minds.

PURITY OF THOUGHT

Malevich was a devout Christian and, like Kandinsky and Mondrian, had mystical beliefs. He said that he wanted his abstract art to give insights into the 'cosmic infinite' and to express 'the supremacy of pure feeling'. About a series of white on white paintings (white forms on white backgrounds) begun in 1918, he proclaimed: 'Fly! A white, free, endlessness – infinity – is before you!' These were abstracts to end all abstracts, but they seem to have been the end of the road for Malevich and total abstraction, as afterwards he returned to representational art.

CONSTRUCTIVISM

The early years of the 20th century were a time of political turmoil in Russia, climaxing in the Revolution of 1917 which saw the overthrow of the Russian king, Tzar Nicholas II, and the birth of a new Communist government.

DOWN WITH FINE ART

This political revolution was accompanied by a revolution in the arts. The group of Russian artists who became known as Constructivists thought that there was no longer any room for old ideas about the superiority of fine arts such as painting and sculpture over applied arts such as furniture and textile design, typography, ceramics and metalworking.

UP WITH TECHNOLOGY

Artists should serve society and be involved in reshaping it, the Constructivists believed. Rather than depicting machines, they should become involved in industrial design and in making things that were socially useful. Varvara Stepanova (1894–1958) and her husband, Alexander Rodchenko (1891–1956), were two of the main leaders of the movement. They proclaimed in 1920, 'Down with art! Up with technology!'

Rodchenko had created Suprematist works for a while in the 1910s, but abandoned easel painting for Constructivism, saying: 'The art of the future will not be the cosy decoration of family homes.' During the '20s he turned instead to photography and design, working on everything from furniture and interiors, to advertizing and propaganda posters. Posters were the chief method of spreading the Communist message to the masses, and thousands were designed and printed after the Revolution.

CONSTRUCTION OF THE USSR
ALEXANDER RODCHENKO, 1920

28

MODEL FOR A MONUMENT TO THE THIRD INTERNATIONAL
VLADIMIR TATLIN, 1919–20
(Reconstructed 1992–93)

Tatlin (1885–1953) was the founder of Constructivism and, although it was never built, his monument was to be made from iron and glass, have revolving sections, and be far taller than the Eiffel Tower.

THE ROAD TO REVOLUTION

Vladimir Ilyich Lenin

The 1917 Revolution began in March, with riots and strikes in St Petersburg. Troops sent to crush the uprising joined it instead, and the Tzar was forced to abdicate. A provisional goverment was set up, but in November the Bolsheviks, led by Lenin (1870–1924), seized power, offering the people 'Bread, peace, land'. In July 1918, the Tzar and his family were executed, almost certainly by Bolsheviks. The Bolsheviks changed the name of their party to the Communist Party of the Soviet Union in the same year.

In 1918–20, the Soviet Union was torn by civil war between Communists and anti-Communists.

GLOSSARY

ABSTRACT ART Art that does not attempt to represent the real world, but which instead expresses meaning or emotion through shapes and colours.

CONSTRUCTIVISM A Russian, geometric abstract art movement that developed just before the Revolution. Artists used industrial materials and tried to break down the gap between fine and applied art.

CUBISM An art style founded by Pablo Picasso and Georges Braque in 1907. Cubist works fragmented the subject into geometric shapes and presented several viewpoints at once.

DADA An anti-sense and anti-tradition movement in art and literature born in Europe and the USA during World War I.

DE STIJL A Dutch, geometric abstract art magazine and movement founded in 1917, which aimed to apply laws of universal harmony to art, life and society.

FUTURISM An Italian art and literature movement founded in 1909, which rejected the past and instead celebrated the dynamism of modern city life and technology. Futurist art was influenced by Orphism.

IMPRESSIONISM A style that originated in the late 1860s, in which artists aimed for impressions of everyday scenes, and tried to capture the fleeting effects of light reflecting off the surface of things.

METAPHYSICAL PAINTING A mysterious, dream-like style of representational painting which developed in Italy in the 1910s.

ORPHISM A colourful abstract and semi-abstract art style, which developed from Cubism in about 1910–12.

PERSPECTIVE The illusion of three-dimensional space and depth created on a flat, two-dimensional surface.

REPRESENTATIONAL ART Art that portrays things seen in the real world. Also known as figurative art.

SUPREMATISM A Russian, geometric abstract art style, which was proclaimed in 1915 in a manifesto by Kasimir Malevich.

VORTICISM A British art and literature movement, which flared briefly into life during the mid-1910s. Vorticist art was influenced by Cubism.

30

WORLD EVENTS

- Union of South Africa founded
- Japan takes control of Korea
- Chinese revolution; Sun Yat Sen establishes republic
- Amundsen reaches South Pole
- Balkan Wars (to '13)
- Titanic sinks on its maiden voyage, with loss of 1,500 people
- Niels Bohr's quantum theory of the structure of the atom published
- Assassination of Austrian Archduke Ferdinand triggers World War I
- ANZAC troops slaughtered on Gallipoli
- UK passenger ship Lusitania torpedoed
- Ireland: Easter Rising in Dublin
- Battles of Verdun and the Somme
- October Revolution in Russia; Lenin takes power
- Brazil & USA declare war on Germany
- Armistice ends World War I
- UK: women over 30 get the vote
- Treaty of Versailles between Allies & Germany
- Germany: Hitler becomes leader of Nazi Party

TIMELINE

	ART	DESIGN	THEATRE & FILM	BOOKS & MUSIC
0	•*Kandinsky paints abstract watercolours* •*London: Fry's first Post-Impressionist exhibition*	•*Adolf Loos' Modernist Steiner House in Vienna* •*Germany: Gropius & Meyer's Fagus shoe factory*	•*New York: Fanny Brice stars in the* Ziegfeld Follies •*Paris: Russian Ballet's* Schéhérazade *&* The Firebird	•*Igor Stravinsky composes music for* The Firebird •*E.M. Forster:* Howards End
1	•*Der Blaue Reiter group formed in Berlin* •*Kandinsky's* On the Spiritual in Art *published*	•*Brussels: J. Hoffmann's Palais Stoclet completed; interior mosaics by Gustav Klimt*	•*Cartoonist Winsor McCay's film* Little Nemo •*Edward Knoblock's play,* Kismet	•*Irving Berlin: 'Alexander's Ragtime Band'* •*Richard Strauss:* Der Rosenkavalier
2	•*Picasso & Braque create first collages* •*R. & S. Delaunay paint totally abstract works*		•*Keystone comedy studio founded by Mack Sennett* •*E. Guazzoni's silent film epic,* Quo Vadis	•*Carl Jung:* The Psychology of the Unconscious •*Arnold Schoenberg:* Pierrot Lunaire
3	•*USA: Armory Show of modern European art* •*Boccioni:* Unique Forms of Continuity in Space	•*Cass Gilbert's gothic-style skyscraper, the Woolworth Building, completed in New York*	•*USA: film studios first set up in Hollywood* •*George Bernard Shaw:* Pygmalion	•*Claude Debussy's* Jeux *for the Russian Ballet* •*D.H. Lawrence:* Sons and Lovers
4	•*BLAST magazine launches Vorticism* •*Bomberg:* The Mud Bath	•*Italy: Antonio Sant'Elia's designs for a Futurist City, Città Nuova*	•*Charlie Chaplin's tramp appears in* Kid Auto Races •*Mack Sennett:* Tillie's Punctured Romance	•*Gustav Holst:* The Planets *(to '17)* •*James Joyce's short stories,* Dubliners
5	•*Malevich publishes his Suprematist manifesto & exhibits geometric abstract paintings*	•*Matte Truco's reinforced concrete Lingotto car factory, Turin, Italy*	•*D.W. Griffith's US civil war epic,* The Birth of a Nation •*Cecil B. De Mille:* The Cheat	•*Death of soldier-poet Rupert Brooke* •*Ford Madox Ford:* The Good Soldier
6	•*Boccioni, Franz Marc & Sant'Elia killed in action* •*Dada born in Cabaret Voltaire, Zurich*	•*E. Johnston's sans serif typeface for the London Underground*	•*Lillian Gish stars in D.W. Griffith's second silent epic,* Intolerance	•*Franz Kafka:* Metamorphosis •*Albert Einstein:* General Theory of Relativity
7	•*Duchamp's ready-made sculpture,* Fountain •*Carrà & de Chirico launch Metaphysical Painting*	•*De Stijl movement founded by van Doesburg & Mondrian*	•*Mary Pickford stars in* The Poor Little Rich Girl •*Charlie Chaplin stars in* The Immigrant	•*Henry Handel Richardson:* Australia Felix •*Erik Satie's* Parade *for the Russian Ballet*
8	•*Malevich's white on white series* •*Death of Klimt*	•*De Stijl designer Gerrit Rietveld's Red and Blue armchair*	•*Vladimir Mayakovsky's pro-revolution play,* Mystery-Bouffe, *first performed in Russia*	•*Booth Tarkington:* The Magnificent Ambersons •*Siegfried Sassoon's anti-war poems,* Counterattack
9	•*Death of Auguste Renoir* •*Mondrian returns to Paris*	•*Bauhaus design school founded in Germany by Walter Gropius*	•*Robert Wiene's Expressionist film,* The Cabinet of Dr Caligari •*United Artists founded*	•*Virginia Woolf:* Night and Day •*André Gide:* Two Symphonies

INDEX

32